You'll Feel Better After You Eat
By
Ellie Perry

Contents

Foreword

Every morning before school, our youngest daughter, Anne, would come downstairs and tell me that she didn't feel well and she couldn't go to school. My response was always, "You'll Feel Better After You Eat"...and she did.

While writing this cookbook, I went back and forth between titles for it, I wanted something that was catchy-something, that would make the reader want to open the book.

The title is but a small part of the stories of my family. The feeling of nostalgia overwhelmed me at times because some of the people that have been important throughout my life are no longer here.

My parents and aunts have been gone for some time so I did the next best thing; I brought them back through the cookbook, through recipes and memories that I shared with them.

Finally, this book is dedicated to our kids, Beth, Laurie, Tom, Joe, and Anne. I hope they share my history with their partners and families, and the next generation.

Buona Fortuna
-Ellie

History

I grew up surrounded by dozens of relatives in a suburb of Chicago. It was an average childhood filled with unconditional love from family and grandparents.

We all lived in the same town or surrounding towns and usually walked up the block or down the street to spend Sundays and holidays with grandparents and relatives.

Today we travel around the world to be with our relatives if we choose. Our children have careers that take them not only across the country, but across the ocean. It is a more sophisticated way of life, and a very exciting time.

Me: Elinore Rochelle Perry

Lenny, Dee, Carol and Me

If we live long enough, most of us will have memories to share with our children, and their children, and so on. I decided to write a cookbook and journal to document my life for the next generation.

I am Italian and steeped in tradition, like most Italian people of my generation, growing up in a close-knit, warm and volatile family. I learned early on that food was one of the most important resources in Italian families. I also learned about tradition within the Italian family. Respect for parents and grandparents, religion, family, and loyalty were things to be acknowledged as very important. The awareness of my parents sacrifice and struggles still touches my heart.

Me, Dee and Carol

My generation grew up in homes without a lot of extras. Money was always tight, yet there was always food on the table. Homemade bread, fresh vegetables from the garden, and bottled fruits that Mom had "put up" for the winter were staples in our diet.

There was no canned food from the grocery store in our home; everything was from the garden. We also had chicken that "resided" in the chicken coop behind the house until Mom needed one for Sunday dinner.

Spaghetti sauce for pasta and other dishes was made from fresh tomatoes. I remember lining the jars up on shelves my dad had made in the basement of our home. What a wonderful gourmet table we had with homegrown eggplant, tomatoes, peppers and fresh corn on the cob. Green beans with new potatoes, and fresh baked bread and pies were made every week. I remember picking cherries and apples with Dee in the backyard and eating as many as we picked.

The worst job I had as a kid was to get eggs from the chicken coop every morning. I used to tell my sister Carol that I was allergic to chicken, but that excuse didn't fly with Dad. I wasn't at all unhappy when the rooster "flew the coop" by way of Dad's chopping block.

One of my most profound memories is of the whole family together, sitting down for coffee and rolls before my dad left to catch the bus for the night shift. Every time I walk by a bakery, I am compelled to stop in, if only to catch the aroma of the fresh bakery smells floating from the back room. We didn't own a car so everything centered on the bus schedule.

Our grandchildren will never have the luxury of hanging around a kitchen table with their parents eating doughnuts or pastries at four o'clock in the afternoon. Their parents barely make it to day care  to pick up the kids before they head home or make the stop to McDonald's or Burger King. The pressures are much different today than they were when I was growing up. We may have had money woes, but life moved at a much slower pace. The simplicity of that era is sadly long gone, along with eating dinner with parents and siblings, playing in an open field at dusk and leaving your doors open at night.

Dee and Me

Our grandchildren don't have the benefits that I had as a child growing up, surrounded by relatives and cousins. I look back on my childhood and am grateful that I lived in that generation. Today, many of the people that I loved are gone, and many are separated by distance, but the memories of that era will live with me forever. What an innocent generation we lived through.

Pasquale, Carol and Me

My brother Lenny has passed on but I still have many memories of how he protected me when I was a small child.

My Dad

I have a wonderful story about my dad. The day before Tony was to go off to the service, I ran into him at A&W Root Beer in Chicago Heights. I had gone to a cook-out and on the way home some friends and I decided to stop for a root beer. I hadn't seen Tony in a while so when I saw him at the stand I ran over to say hello. I suggested to him that he come over to my home so we could visit before he

left the next day. When my friends dropped me off at home, I simply jumped out of their car and jumped into Tony's car. We went for a ride and decided that it would be nice to write to each other.

Little did I know that Dad had been watching me move from one car to the other! When I got out of Tony's car after our ride, I saw Dad's silhouette in the window, and I knew I was in trouble.

I figured if I could make it into the bathroom before Dad stopped me, I would be okay. I made it to the bathroom just as he was rounding the corner from the kitchen. After I set my hair, unset it, and reset it again, I thought the coast was clear, so I opened the door to step out of the bathroom. There sat Dad waiting for me. He

issued an ultimatum. He said that while I lived in his home, I could date whomever I wanted, one at a time. I could not however, date George Spitz, Pat Soucie, and Tony Perry at the same time. That was not acceptable to him.

In those days we didn't leave home and live in apartments. We left home to get married...period. Ironically, and without any knowledge of what he had done, Dad helped me to make up my mind to begin a "courtship" with Tony that has lasted almost fifty years. *Hey, wait a minute...maybe he really **DID** know what he was doing!*

4

Dad grew up in Foggia, Italy in the region of Apulia near the Adriatic Sea. His family home was in a mountainous area where grapes grew throughout the region. He was raised by very strict parents along with his brothers and his sister, Caroline. My Dad, Leonard, was very adventurous. He wanted desperately to come to America, so when he was seventeen years old, he boarded a ship along

with many other immigrants and crossed the sea, docking in Canada. When he left his homeland, his mom had given him a trunk for his bride-to-be, whom he hadn't yet met. The trunk contained beautiful handmade linens with heavy embroidered lace tablecloths, napkins, and handmade sheets. Unfortunately, halfway through the United States, he had to leave his trunk behind because it was too difficult to hop freight trains with the extra baggage.

He stayed in New York for a short time before hopping a freight train out of the Big Apple. Dad traveled from one coast to the other, stopping for a period of time in Fresno, California. He loved that

area, and later on in life, tried to convince my mom to move to California. It reminded him of his homeland with fresh fruits, vegetables, and friendly people. Unfortunately, he never returned to his home and he never saw his sister again. Years later, after his death, my mom traveled to Italy to meet with Aunt Caroline.

My Mom

Mom worked in a factory during the Second World War, packaging wiring for a business called Diamond Wire Company. She worked the seven to three shift with all of her lady friends. Dad worked the evening shift so the only time that we could be all together was when Mom finished her shift. Because we didn't own a car, she would stop at Schranz Bakery for rolls and donuts before she caught the bus home. She would walk the mile home from the bus stop, where Dad would be waiting for her with the metal coffeepot perking on the stove. Everything stopped at that time so we could all sit down and enjoy the coffee and rolls. I vividly remember my mom getting off the bus with bags of groceries and lugging the groceries home. One of us kids was always with her to help, but I realize now how difficult it must have been for her.

In Mom's lifetime she worked in a factory, as a dishwasher in a restaurant, and in her later years she was assistant to the librarian at Prairie State College in Chicago Heights. She worked there through her seventies. She never gave up even when her health was weakening and she was unable to see. Diabetes had wreaked havoc on her and really took its toll in the early ninties.

My parents tried to provide their kids with a strong sense of commitment, even when things were bleak and money was not readily available for them. Hopefully, they passed their strength and determination on to me.

Aunt Connie

Of all Mom's sisters, Aunt Jennie was the best cook. She could make everything taste wonderful. I can remember eating tomatoes and eggs, peppers and eggs, fried dough, and fried dandelion greens that she and Aunt Connie prepared for us. Joanne, Elaine, Dee, and I would go with the aunts to pick dandelions, blueberries, and strawberries from the fields. That was the good part. The bad part was that we usually had to help clean and can all the "stuff" that we picked. We all climbed into the back of one of the aunt's cars or trucks and went dandelion picking. There was no social barometer reminding us of who we were and how we should act. We just had a fun time.

Aunt Connie, Aunt Jennie, and my mom lived in Chicago Heights, and Aunt Grace and Aunt Angeline lived in the Chicago area, but they called each other almost every day and managed to see each other once a week. How lucky they were! If one of the aunts found a good recipe or made a special dish, it was shared with whomever lived close to their home.

Mom and Her Sisters

This group of sisters shopped together, vacationed together, and sometimes ate together, and yet never had a argument that threatened their relationship. Looking back on that era, they seemed to have the same issues with their parents as we had with ours in the fifties and probably as our kids will have with their kids, and so on.

Growing up in the fifties

Dee and I, waiting for our dates

Claire, Dee, Bonnie, Joanne, Isabelle, and Me

Enjoying food at the Italian Village, Chicago

Flirting with the waiters, acting crazy

When my sister Dee and I were in high school, we hung around together. Or I should say she and her friends let me tag along with them. I was two years younger than them, but we had a good time together. We all worked either at a local restaurant chopping salads, or some of the girls worked in their family restaurants. After graduating from Bloom High School, four of us went to work at a bank in Chicago Heights, Illinois. True to our generation of women, we worked at a bank for two years, and then we married the guy we went with in high school. The fifties generation had three goals: get married, buy a house, and have kids. Before we got married, we did many things together. We would get all dressed up on a Friday or Saturday with our three-inch heels and our white gloves and take a train to Chicago, or Bonnie would drive us in her car. She always drove; she was the only one who had a car. We would either go to dinner at the Italian Village or go to see celebrities perform at the Oriental Theatre. Then we would walk through the park. **Walk through the park?** I hear you ask. It was the fifties and it was pretty safe to walk anywhere in those days.

Italian Cookery

Contrary to certain popular belief, Italy is the Mother of Continental European cookery. Dating back to the ancient Romans, Italy's fame in the culinary field came long before that of France. Although French cookery has taken on its own characteristics, it grew to some degree directly from the Italians.

Italian dishes are purely traditional, and have been influenced very little by the cultures of other countries. Many popular foods such as vegetables, salad greens, and wines were used in the days of Nero in much the same way as in present-day Italy.

The bases of the most colorful Italian dishes are tomatoes, garlic and olive oil. Yet, foods in Italy are as diverse as they are traditional. It is not at all unusual to find an Italian who likes neither tomato sauce nor garlic, he probably has his spaghetti with a butter and cheese sauce and prefers melon and prosciutto to an ordinary antipasto course.

From the Alps to Sicily, from the rice and polenta in the North, to the tomato and eggplant in the South, these recipes are designed to bring pleasure to the recipients of this cookbook.

Appetizers and Soups

The parade of Italian food sometimes begins with the antipasto or "before the meal" course. The varied regions and seasons control what is included in the starter course. Maybe it will include prosciutto and cantaloupe or a few vegetables, or bite-size appetizers, such as meats, cheeses, raw vegetables and pickled varieties of vegetables. This is the introduction to the meal.

After the antipasto comes the soup. Each region in Italy has its own distinct soups. From minestrone, which is a meal in itself, to soups with macaroni or rice, this becomes the first main course. I have included three soups that my family has enjoyed throughout our history, and still enjoys today.

Fresh Tomato Bruschetta

4 medium tomatoes, chopped	salt and pepper to taste
¼ cup fresh chopped basil	3 cloves garlic, chopped
6 tablespoons olive oil	garlic bread rounds

Place the chopped tomatoes with their juices and the oil in a small bowl. Season the mixture with salt and pepper. Stir in basil and chopped garlic. Store in the refrigerator to blend juices.
Serve with garlic bread rounds.*

*You can purchase garlic/parmesan rounds of bread in specialty stores or in selected grocery stores.

Italian Giblets and Mushrooms with Peas and Carrots – An Italian Tradition

5lbs. chicken giblets	1 cup white wine
1 stick butter, not margarine	½ cup water
oil to cover bottom of pan	2 cups chopped mushrooms
4 cloves garlic, minced	½ cup parsley, minced
1 cup chopped celery with leaves	1 large can tomato sauce

Soak the gizzards thoroughly in water and drain. Cut gizzards in small pieces, removing tendon nerves. Place in large pan and cover with water. Bring to boil. Skim the film that forms on top. Boil until tender (about 20 minutes) Drain. Meanwhile, in a large skillet, heat oil and ¼ cup of butter. Brown the gizzards lightly. Add tomatoes, garlic, and celery with leaves, parsley, salt and pepper to taste. Mix thoroughly. Simmer on low heat while you sauté the rest of the ingredients.

In another skillet, sauté 4 tablespoons of butter, add mushrooms and sauté until mushrooms are slightly golden brown. Add mushrooms and butter to giblet mixture and simmer slowly until giblets are tender and the sauce is cooked. (About 45 minutes)

This traditional Italian dish is not one that most people would try for a dinner party. I included this dish because it is such an important part of our tradition. This was served at every Italian wedding in Chicago Heights and it is delicious. Our grandson Braden calls them "Giglets". Giblets can be found in the chicken section of your grocery store.

13

Caponata Appetizer

The leader in the parade of Italian Appetizers is the antipasto or "before the meal" course. We know the antipasto as fresh sliced meats, cheeses, olives and Italian sausage chunks. The antipasto course varies from region to region and from season to season. It varies from prosciutto wrapped around a slice of melon; a crisp vegetable attractively presented in a large tray, or stuffed artichokes, one of my favorites.

Caponata is the Italian version of ratatouille. It is prepared similarly and tastes similar, but it can be prepared in advance and eaten cold.

Add some chunks of long, narrow Italian bread or garlic rounds and you have a wonderful introduction to lunch or dinner.

Preparing Caponata

2 firm eggplants
½ cup olive oil
3 stalks celery, chopped
2 large red peppers, diced
2 large green peppers, diced
4 tomatoes, chopped
1 cup green-pitted olives
1 cup black-pitted olives
2 tablespoons diced garlic
1 teaspoon oregano
1 cup red wine vinegar
salt and pepper to taste

Wash eggplant and cut lengthwise in cubes. Heat oil in large frying pan and sauté celery and red and green pepper over low heat until tender. Add eggplant and remaining ingredients.

Simmer uncovered until all the ingredients are tender, but not mushy. Stir often and cook on low heat for about 35 minutes.

Serve as appetizer with garlic rounds or small slices of Italian bread.

This is a great appetizer for a group. It presents beautifully and serves a lot of people.

Chicken Soup with Dumplings

1 x 3 to 4lb. Chicken	3 stalks celery, chopped	4 carrots, chopped
1 medium onion	1 bunch escarole, chopped	salt and pepper to taste

In large pot, cover chicken with cold water and bring to a boil. Skim the foam that forms on the surface. Chop the onion, carrots and celery and thoroughly wash and chop the escarole. Add the vegetables to the soup and reduce heat. Simmer for approximately 2 hours or until chicken is falling from the bone. Remove the chicken from the soup and cool. Detach all the chicken from the bone, cut into chunks then add 2 cups of chicken to soup. Depending on the size of the chicken, save the remaining chicken for Chicken Ala King or Chicken Pie.

Adding Dumplings after soup is done:

1 cup flour	½ cup milk	½ teaspoon salt
2 tablespoons oil	1½ teaspoons baking powder	

Sift flour, salt and baking powder. Add milk and salad oil. This makes soft dough. Stir well and drop from spoon onto soup. Cover tightly and steam without lifting cover for 15 minutes. If you are in a hurry, you can make the dumplings from the recipe on the side of the Bisquick box.

Pasta e Fagioli Soup

2 large bunches chopped escarole, washed thoroughly and squeezed dry

2 x 14oz. cans low sodium chicken broth

1cup elbow macaroni

2 x 15oz. cans cannelloni beans with juice

½ cup olive oil

1 x 8oz. can tomato sauce

4 garlic cloves, chopped

Salt and pepper to taste

Coarsely chop escarole and squeeze out extra water. In a large pot, brown 2 cloves chopped garlic in ¼ cup oil. Add escarole and sauté for 10 minutes. Add chicken broth and beans with juice. Mix well and simmer on stove for 10 minutes. Meanwhile, in a separate skillet sauté 2 cloves chopped garlic in ¼ cup olive oil on low heat until golden brown. Add tomato sauce, salt and pepper. Simmer over low heat for 10 minutes while you prepare the macaroni. Cook pasta al dente as directed on box. When done, drain thoroughly and add to the soup mix. Add tomato sauce from skillet and simmer on low heat until all the flavors are blended, approximately 15 minutes. Stir frequently so beans do not stick to bottom of pot. Top soup with grated Romano cheese. Serve piping hot with chunks of Italian bread. Serve immediately because the pasta can swell and absorb all of the soup.

Butternut Squash Soup

4 tablespoons unsalted butter or olive oil

2 large diced onions

1 teaspoon nutmeg

½ teaspoon ground cinnamon

½ teaspoon pumpkin spice

10 cups peeled and diced butternut squash (2 to 3 squash)

10 cups chicken stock

salt and pepper to taste

Melt butter or heat oil in large pot over medium heat. Add onions and cook until tender. Stir in spices, cooking for 1 minute and then add chicken stock and squash. Bring to boil, then reduce heat and simmer uncovered until squash is very tender. Cool for a few minutes, then remove squash from pot and place in food processor or blender to process. Add a little stock with the batches of squash. Add enough stock for a medium thick soup. Reserve any leftover stock because the soup thickens as it stands. Season with salt and pepper. Serve piping hot.

This soup is perfect for fall when the weather gets a little nippy.

Savoia's Antipasto

6 thin slices prosciutto

6 thin slices mortadella

6 slices pepperoni sausage

½ lb. cooked Italian sausage cut in ¾ inch pieces

6 kalamata olives

6 wedges fontina cheese

6 slices supresatta salami

6 slices Genoa salami

6 marinated artichoke hearts

6 slices provolone cheese

6 large green pitted olives

6 fresh jumbo shrimp

Using a large tray or platter, line the bottom with crisp lettuce leaves. Arrange all the ingredients. Serve with garlic rounds or chunky Italian bread. For variation, you can add tomatoes, giardiniera, green onions and celery hearts.

This antipasto is very popular at a buffet table. It presents beautifully and can be made a day before a party and stored in the refrigerator. The salamis and Italian meats can be purchased at any Italian market and selected grocery stores.

Bread, Pizza and Pizza Frite

Hard-crusted bread; complicated fancy Easter bread, crunchy bread sticks and varied pizza breads are among the most traditional foods in Italian cookery.

The expression, "earning one's bread and wine" is taken literally in Italy where a dinner may consist of only bread, soup and wine. The Italians especially enjoy hard, crusty bread, whether spread with ricotta cheese at breakfast, or oil and garlic at dinner, or taken as a half loaf for lunch. They often remove the soft center of the bread and eat only the crunchy, crisp outside crust.

Aunt Jennie's Pizza Frite:
Place 6 cups flour in large mixing bowl. Mix together 1 package dry yeast, ¼ cup warm water and 1 teaspoon sugar. Place in center well of flour. Also add 1 teaspoon salt, 1 tablespoon Crisco, 2 cups lukewarm water. Knead well, adding flour when needed. Cover dough in oven and let rise until doubled. Meanwhile heat ¼ cup canola oil in large fry pan. Break off large pieces of dough (the size of an egg) and stretch dough. Place dough in heated oil and brown on both sides. Drain on paper towels. Sprinkle cinnamon/sugar on frittels, or spread butter and serve immediately. This same recipe can be used to make pizza dough.

Grandma Rendina's Bread

5lb. of Gold Medal Flour	3 teaspoon salt
2 packages of dry yeast	3 eggs, beaten
½ cup vegetable oil	5¼ cups warm water

Dissolve the yeast in ¼ cup warm water. Mix flour and salt together. Make a well in the flour and salt mixture. Add additional water, oil and beaten eggs. Mix all ingredients well. Knead until everything is blended. Cover with dishtowel. Put in warm place to rise. When dough has doubled in size, punch down and let rise to double in size again. Punch down again. Form into loaves or for pizzas. Bake at 375 degrees for 45 minutes until golden brown.

The same dough can be used for pizza. For pizza, bake for 20 minutes until bubbly.

This recipe makes 5 loaves of bread or 3 pizzas or 2 loaves of bread, 3 pans of dinner rolls and fried Pizza Frita (fried dough)

This is the original recipe from my mom and passed down to my sister Dee and me.

Mom's Fried Dough

My mom made this wonderful fried dough, called Frittels or Pizza Frite, when she made bread every week. Mom would stretch the dough and fry it in the large cast-iron frying pan; and after draining it on paper towels, we would slather the fried dough with butter and then sprinkle cinnamon and sugar on top. In later years Aunt Jennie and Aunt Connie would make this when I would visit them.

When we traveled to Italy, we stopped at a café in the Piazza Navona, ordered fried dough and walked down the narrow streets munching it. I felt like I was back in my mom's kitchen eating her wonderful Frittels.

Olive, Tomato, Spinach and Pepper Pizza

½ red pepper

½ green bell pepper

1 small can whole tomatoes, mashed into small pieces or 2 to 3 fresh, ripe mashed tomatoes

10 black pitted olives, sliced

½ box frozen chopped spinach, squeezed dry

1 large package of shredded mozzarella cheese

Chopped fresh basil (optional)

Grandma Rendina's bread recipe or Aunt Jennie's Frittel recipe

Pour ¼ cup light olive oil in bottom of frying pan. Heat on medium heat. Place mashed tomatoes in oil and simmer on stove for about 5 minutes. Add chopped spinach, olives and pepper and sauté until tender.

Meanwhile place a thin layer of mozzarella cheese on the pizza shell. Spoon mixed vegetables with tomato on top of cheese. Spread on pizza shell, leaving room on the edges of pizza. Top with more mozzarella cheese. Bake at 425 degrees until cheese bubbles and crust is golden brown. Allow the pizza to sit for a few minutes before cutting. Enjoy!

Follow the recipe from Grandma Rendina's bread. For pizza, stretch and roll out your dough to form a circle. I use a large round pizza pan with low sides and then I fit the dough by pressing down on the sides to make a circle. You have to do a little stretching and pulling. You can also use a rectangular pan or a jellyroll pan.

I have used a plain tomato sauce for the topping of one pizza, and a vegetable topping for the second pizza. You can also add chunks of Italian sausage, pepperoni or other meats to the topping. Mom and Dad always used fresh tomatoes. To do this, break apart the whole tomato into small pieces. For cheese pizza, place the tomatoes on the dough and top with cheese and basil. Bake at 425 degrees until cheese is bubbling and brown on top.

What could be better than homemade pizza and a cool beer on a Friday night? Or any other night for that matter!

At an open market in Rome, Italy 1995

Vegetables

"Part of the secret of success in life is to eat what you like and let the food fight it out inside."

Mark Twain

Stuffed Artichokes

4 artichokes

salt to taste

3 to 4 tablespoons of oil drizzled over top of artichokes before cooking

mix together the stuffing:

1½ cups Italian breadcrumbs

1 teaspoon salt

pepper to taste

1 tablespoon parsley, minced

1 clove garlic, minced

½ cup or more olive oil to moisten the breadcrumb mixture

Preparing the Artichokes

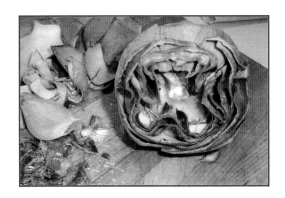

Wash and trim artichokes. Cut off the outer leaves that are tough and separate the leaves. Remove as much of the choke at the bottom of the artichoke as you can. This is the prickly part at the bottom of the artichoke. Also trim the tops of the leaves that have prickly edges. After you have mixed the stuffing, tuck bits between the leaves. You can be generous, but do not stuff the leaves too full. You will have to spread the leaves apart to get the stuffing in securely.

Cut the stem of the artichoke straight, so that it stands up in the pan. Place in large saucepan with about 2 inches of water; but do not cover the artichoke. Drizzle about 3 to 4 tablespoons of olive oil over top. Cover the artichokes and cook about 2 hours on low heat or until the leaves pull apart easily.

Use as an appetizer or a side dish.

Eggplant Parmesan
Light version

2 to 3 large eggplants	1 large package of shredded mozzarella cheese
salt	¼ to ½ cup olive oil to coat the eggplant
2½ cups marinara sauce (p.69)	

Cut the eggplant in round slices. Drain the eggplant in a colander for 30 minutes. Place the eggplant on a cookie sheet sprayed with cooking spray. Lay the eggplant in single layers on cookie sheet and brush the top of the eggplant with olive oil. Place in the oven at 325 degrees and brown on both sides. Repeat until all of the eggplant is used. Pat dry on paper towels. Watch the eggplant closely so it does not burn.

Spread a thin layer of marinara sauce in a shallow 9x13 baking dish. Add a layer of eggplant slices, overlapping slightly. Top with a layer of mozzarella, another layer of sauce, and a sprinkle of grated cheese. Repeat, ending with eggplant, sauce, and mozzarella.

Bake at 350 degrees, or until sauce is bubbling and the cheese is melted. Let stand for 10 minutes before serving.

Eggplant Parmesan
Traditional version

2 medium eggplant

2 eggs, beaten

2 tablespoons water

½ cup bread crumbs

marinara sauce (p.69)

½ teaspoon oregano

½ cup grated Romano cheese

8 cups shredded mozzarella cheese

oil for frying

Cut the eggplant in round slices. Drain the eggplant in colander for 30 minutes. Dip eggplant into egg mixture, then into crumbs. Sauté in oil until brown and tender.

Drain on paper towels. In lightly greased 9x13 Pyrex pan, place enough sauce to cover bottom of pan. Add one layer of fried eggplant, overlapping slightly, and then add a layer of mozzarella cheese. Repeat with sauce, eggplant and cheese, ending with sauce. Sprinkle Parmesan cheese over the top. Bake in 350-degree oven for 30 to 40 minutes.

This traditional version is excellent but quite heavy. If you love Eggplant Parmesan like I do and you have some health issues, you might want to try the lighter version.

Italians love the land and because they do there is no shortage of fresh and delicious vegetables in Italy. When I was growing up in Chicago Heights, every Italian on the block had a vegetable garden. My chore every day in the summer was to pull the weeds in the garden. Fresh corn on the cob was picked and eaten that day, tomatoes were picked ripe from the vine, washed and eaten as a snack. There was no shortage of vegetables in our home. My mom and dad used the vegetables in many imaginative and varied ways. Because meat was expensive for our family, vegetables took the place of the meat for many of our meals.

In Italy and in our home, I buy when the vegetables are in season and at their best. For summer eating, I have learned to take advantage of the farmers' markets and stands for fresh picked vegetables. Of course I use canned tomatoes for sauce, but in the summer when tomatoes are at their peak, I like to use fresh tomatoes for sauce.

One of my friends once asked me why I didn't use the Cuisinart that Tony had bought for me in the 1980's. I replied that I like handling the vegetables. Maybe it reflects back to my youth and picking vegetables from the garden. My kitchen area looks out directly into the morning and afternoon sun. I can see my flowers, the flowering tree in the front yard, the baseball field and people coming up the driveway. It is the sunniest room in our home and a real delight to prepare food and to chop vegetables in all that cheerfulness.

Cauliflower, Eggplant and Zucchini

1 cauliflower
1 small eggplant
1 zucchini
3 eggs, beaten
½ cup milk
2 cups all-purpose flour
salt and pepper to taste
Canola oil for frying

You will need a deep fryer or cast-iron skillet.

Wash vegetables thoroughly. Cut the core from the cauliflower. It is easier to break apart the "flower" of the cauliflower. Break into medium-sized pieces and set aside. Meanwhile slice the eggplant and zucchini in lengthwise slices. Set aside. In large bowl, beat eggs and milk together. In a separate bowl, add flour. Dip vegetables in milk and egg mixture, then in the flour. Coat the vegetables a few at a time and fry in deep fryer. Your deep fryer must be hot in order for the vegetables to "crisp". Cook in batches. When crisp, place on paper towels and pat off extra oil. Arrange in large platter and serve. This cauliflower was always served on Christmas Eve when I was a child. It is delicious and worth the time and effort.

Green Beans and Potatoes

2lbs. fresh green beans

6 new red potatoes, peeled and cut in chunks

½ cup olive oil

salt and pepper to taste

2 cloves chopped garlic, optional

Wash and drain beans. Snip off the ends of the beans. Place in boiling water and cook until crisp. You don't want to overcook beans because they get mushy and the color turns a light green. While beans are cooking, peel potatoes and place in water to boil. Cook the potatoes until firm, but not soft, approximately 20 to 25 minutes. Drain the potatoes. When the beans are cooked, strain well. Place warm beans and potatoes in a large bowl. Pour oil over top, add salt and pepper to taste and mix well. The flavors need to blend together so make this early in the day. They can be served at room temperature.

Roasted Red Peppers with Garlic

Our son-in-law Dan loves to cook. In fact he has pretty much taken over the kitchen at their home. He loves garlic as does Beth, Nicholas and Braden.

One day as I was leaving their home he gave me some roasted red peppers to take home. They had so much garlic in them that my eyes were watering when I ate them, but they were delicious. Fortunately, I can eat garlic, but if Tony, Joe, Anne or Laurie had eaten the peppers, we would have had to double the "little purple pill" for them.

As I said earlier in the cookbook, not all Italians eat garlic.

Preparing the Peppers

Heat oven to 425 degrees. Place the peppers in a cast-iron frying pan or roaster with low side and roast until partially charred, turning frequently. Remove from roaster and place in pot with tight-fitting cover until cool.

Carefully remove the seeds and the "vein" of the peppers with a small butter knife.

Cut in medium strips and place in bowl. Coarsely chop 2 cloves of garlic and add to peppers. Pour ¼ cup olive oil over peppers and mix. Arrange the peppers on a small platter and chill.

Stuffed Peppers

4 large bell peppers

1 lb. ground chuck

1 egg

1 tablespoon grated Parmesan cheese

½ cup cooked rice

salt and pepper to taste

6 tablespoons olive oil

1 8 oz. can Hunts tomato sauce

2 teaspoons basil

1 teaspoon parsley

Wash, core and remove seeds from peppers. Salt insides lightly. Combine meat, egg, cheese, rice, salt, pepper, and parsley. Fill peppers. Place in baking dish. Heat oil in saucepan and add tomato sauce and basil. Simmer for about 10 minutes and pour over peppers. Bake in moderate oven at 350 degrees until peppers are tender. Baste several times while baking.

Serve with chunks of Italian bread and tossed salad. Add a glass of wine and enjoy!

Oven Roasted Peppers and Potatoes

I sometimes add either chicken or Italian sausage to my vegetables and then roast everything together. Total cooking time is usually 45 minutes with the meat and vegetables. The beauty of this recipe is that it is so easy and presents so beautifully on a buffet table.

Preheat oven to 350 degrees. Meanwhile scrub well 6 red unpeeled potatoes, and quarter them. Place ½ cup olive oil in bottom of roasting pan and place in oven to heat. Cut 6 peppers, removing seeds and vein of pepper. Mix peppers and potatoes, place in heated pan in oven and roast for about 30 minutes, until the potatoes and peppers are tender when tested with fork. Shake the pan occasionally to redistribute the vegetables. Do not salt the potatoes until the end of cooking because they get too soft if you salt them too soon. Resist the urge to turn the potatoes too often.

Roasted Vegetables with Sausage

2 new red potatoes scrubbed clean

1 each-red, green and yellow pepper, seeded and sliced

1 eggplant sliced lengthwise

1 zucchini sliced lengthwise

¼ cup oil for roasting

salt and pepper to taste

In a large roasting pan with low sides, place the vegetables in oil, stirring to coat the vegetables. Roast for approximately 20 minutes. Meanwhile on stovetop, sear the sausage to brown, approximately 10 minutes. Try not to poke the sausage because you want to retain the juices. When sausage is brown on both sides, remove from pan and place in roasting pan along with vegetables. Continue to roast at 325 degrees for 20 minutes or until vegetables are crisp. Stir occasionally. Serve with hard rolls or on buffet table with other Italian dishes.

I have on occasion placed sausage, peppers and potatoes in a roaster and cooked them together, however, the potatoes and peppers brown more evenly when I prepare them separately. You can double or triple the recipe depending on the quantity of people you are serving.

My family spent a lot of time at Lenny and Avis' when they were younger. We shared recipes and ate dinner at their home many times. She is a very good cook, as was Lenny.

One year, shortly after Tom was born, Avis, her four kids, along with my kids and I went to a cottage in Hesperia, Michigan. Tony and I had gone there with Ed and Lila Blondell, so I was familiar with the area. However, I misjudged the distance to Hesperia from Chicago Heights. It took us seven hours by car to get to our destination. We had playpens, buggies, toys, food, and formula for Tom, and the all-important pacifier for Trina. However, we did forget one important thing: A clock. So all week when we were going in for lunch and giving our kids a nap, the other guests were coming out for their morning swim at the lake. We noticed that nobody was ever out at the lake when we were there, but we assumed the other guests were busy elsewhere. Turns out we were probably getting up at 5:30 a.m. to swim, and coming into lunch and naptime at 9:30 in the morning.

Finally, toward the end of the week, we turned on the radio in the car to get the weather report and heard the announcer give the time. We were so embarrassed at our foolishness; we left the next day for home and never went back to Hesperia again. Trina lost her pacifier on the way home and cried for a straight five hours. We tried to give her a new one, but she wanted her "broken in" pacifier.

Avis' Cabbage Rolls

1 head green cabbage

1½ cups water

½ teaspoon salt

1 cup instant white rice

2 tablespoons olive oil

1 small onion, chopped

1 lb. lean ground beef

2 tablespoons parsley

Soak the cabbage in cold water for about 10 minutes. This will loosen the leaves. Core the cabbage deeply. Meanwhile fill a pot ¾ full of water and bring to boil. Immerse the cored cabbage into the water and cook, turning occasionally until the leaves are translucent, about 15 minutes. Lift the cabbage out to cool. When the cabbage is cool, remove the outer leaves very carefully. If the leaves are still too hard, return to the water and cook a little longer. You will need about 15 leaves in all. Place the cooled leaves on the counter to be filled.

Cook the rice according to directions. In a frying pan, heat the oil, adding the onion. Cook until soft. Transfer the onion to a large bowl and add the rice, beef, parsley, salt and pepper. After you have placed 2 or 3 tablespoons of filling in each cabbage leaf, fold the sides in and roll up. Place the cabbage rolls seam side down. Pour a little of the tomato sauce over the cabbage roll, cover with foil and bake until the leaves are tender, approximately 1 to 1¼ hours at 350 degrees.

Sauce for Cabbage Rolls:

To make the sauce for the rolls, place ¼ cup of olive oil in frying pan to heat. Add 1 x 15oz. can Hunts Tomato Sauce, salt and pepper and simmer for about 20 minutes on medium high. Add ½ can water from the tomato sauce can and continue to simmer for 10 minutes. Serve with chunks of Italian bread. You may want to double the recipe for the sauce to pour over the rolls when they are served.

Greens with Pancetta

4 large bunches of endive

salt and pepper to taste

1 package of Pancetta (Italian bacon)

garlic

In a large pot, boil water. Meanwhile, wash the endive 3 or 4 times in cold water. Endive retains sand and dirt particles so wash it thoroughly. When the water comes to a rolling boil, add the endive. Use a large wooden spoon to push the endive down so that it is covered by water. Cook over medium low heat until done, approximately 10 to 15 minutes. You don't want the endive to become mushy, so use the same policy as you would with pasta al dente. Drain well and cool. Squeeze out any extra liquid using your hands.

Place about 4 slices of pancetta in a frying pan. Do not add oil. Brown until crisp. Remove the pancetta from pan to cool. Slice in small pieces. Add a small amount of olive oil to same frying pan and add the well-drained endive. Cook for about 10 minutes. Place in a large serving platter, adding the browned pancetta on top. Serve at room temperature.

Recently our daughter Laurie and her husband, Dennis, had a dinner party and served this along with a wonderful beef tenderloin and other dishes. While the whole menu was delicious, the guests raved over Laurie's greens with pancetta. It's not your usual vegetable, but it can be prepared well before a dinner party and either served at room temperature or heated right before the dinner.

40

Candied Sweet Potatoes

These are the best! We usually spent Thanksgiving at Mary Jo and Aunt Katherine's home when the kids were younger and these potatoes were always served. Thanksgiving wouldn't have been complete without this wonderful side dish.

The secret to the glaze is to make sure that the dark brown sugar, white sugar; cinnamon, butter and orange juice all blend well before you coat the potatoes.

To coat the potatoes, place one potato at a time in the brown sugar mixture on the stove and coat each side of the potato. After you have coated each potato, place them in a 9x13 Pyrex glass baking dish and spoon the remaining brown sugar mix over the potatoes. Use the sauce liberally. Bake at 375 degrees and then let the potatoes cool a little so that the glaze hardens on the potatoes. My kids love these. If you are making these the day before serving, they need to be heated for about 30 minutes.

5 sweet potatoes, uniform in size

1 box dark brown sugar

1 tablespoon cinnamon

1/4 lb. butter, not margarine

¼ cup water

1/4 cup white sugar

Cover potatoes with water, and boil till tender when poked with a knife. Do not over boil potatoes. Cool, peel and set aside. When they are completely cool, slice lengthwise.

In the meantime, in a large skillet, dissolve both sugars in 1/4-cup water. Boil until thread is formed (drizzle from a spoon). Add cinnamon and stick of butter. After the sugar solution is at the right consistency, place cooled potatoes in the skillet and coat each side.

Place the potatoes in a buttered 9x13 casserole and pour the sauce over them. Try to get enough sauce on each one. You may have to use 2 Pyrex pans. Bake at 350 degrees about 40-45 min. or until browned.

Beef, Poultry and Fish

Italians prepare their meats, poultry, fish and sauces differently in each region.

In Naples you will find veal cutlets cut thin for Veal Scaloppini or Veal Marsala. In a kitchen in Rome you can smell the frying of Frito Misto, which combines vegetables and fish. Along the seacoast, Lobster Fra Diavolo or Shrimp Scampi is the dish. Travel to southern Italy and you will find chicken pieces cooking in bubbly tomato sauce for Chicken Cacciatore.

Tuscany 2002

An Italian family who winters in Clearwater, Florida and spends their summers at business at their villa in Tuscany invited us for lunch. Their nephew was our tour guide.

The hostess generously labeled all the food on the buffet so the "English" would understand what each dish was and its origin. Lunch was served on their terrace beneath the vast sweep of the Alps. After climbing winding roads on our huge tour bus, we arrived at their gorgeous villa. The incredible view from the villa took our breath away, as did the curving ride up and down on the bus.

Roast Chicken with Potatoes, Peppers and Olives in Wine Sauce

This is one of the easiest dishes to prepare, not only for your family, but also if you are having guests. It is roasted together in the oven using one large roasting pan with low sides or a Pyrex glass baking dish.

2 each: green and red peppers, sliced, seeds removed   ½ cup olive oil

1 chicken, cut in pieces   ½ cup white wine

6 small red potatoes cut in half   ¼ cup water

12 kalamata olives

Place chicken, peppers, and potatoes in roasting pan with low sides. Pour oil over top of chicken and vegetables and stir to coat. Place in oven to bake. Roast at 375 degrees for 60 minutes or until golden brown. Mix together the olives, wine and water and add to chicken for the last 10 minutes. Remove pieces of chicken to serving platter. Pat the chicken with paper towel to remove extra oil from top. On top of stove simmer wine, water and drippings to blend, stirring frequently. Before serving, drizzle wine sauce over chicken.

44

Chicken Spezzato

16 pieces of chicken

2 cloves garlic, cut in pieces

2 stalks of celery cut in half

2 x 4oz. cans mushroom pieces

1 cup olive oil*

1 tablespoon rosemary leaves

1 cup white wine

1 tablespoon parsley

Place chicken in a large skillet or roasting pan with low sides. Pour the cup of oil over the chicken; turning pieces of chicken to coat them. Brown the chicken on both sides on stove. When chicken is brown, remove from skillet. Place in roasting pan in oven adding ¼ cup of oil from skillet, garlic, celery, mushroom pieces, parsley, and crushed rosemary leaves. Roast for ½ hour at 375 degrees. If there is an excessive amount of liquid from the chicken, drain some of it, leaving a small amount in the roasting pan. Pour the wine over the chicken and lower heat down to 350 degrees. Cook for 1 hour. Remove from pan and arrange on serving platter.

The blended flavors from the garlic, rosemary and wine make this a delicious entrée.

*You can use light oil if you prefer. It is a lot of oil, but you drain most of the oil after the chicken is roasted, then add the wine.

Rack of Lamb

Rack of Lamb is really special in every sense of the word. Tony loves it prepared any way possible. The smaller the rib chops the better. People object to lamb because of the strong flavor of the meat, but trust me, this is the filet of lamb. When preparing, simply roast in a hot oven or place on your grill for about 20 to 30 minutes. You want to have the outside slightly charred and the inside medium rare. Plan on three rib widths per person. Served with mint jelly, it is a beautiful dinner entrée.

Preparation: 2 racks of lamb untrimmed

salt and pepper

Preheat oven or grill to 425 degrees. Rub salt and pepper over lamb. If preparing in oven, place in open roasting pan, using the ribs as a rack. Lay directly on rack for grilling. Roast uncovered for 20 to 30 minutes. A meat thermometer should register 135 to 140 degrees. Remove and let cool before carving.

Braciole

2 thin slices round steak, (use meat hammer to tenderize)

1 cup grated Romano cheese   3 cloves garlic, minced

salt and pepper to taste   3 tablespoon fresh parsley

oil to fry steak   1½ cups breadcrumbs

1 small onion, chopped   1 tablespoon fresh basil

2 cloves garlic, whole

Spread cheese heavily over meat, leaving edges dry. Sprinkle breadcrumbs, minced garlic, parsley, salt, and pepper over cheese in layers. Roll meat as you would a jellyroll. Tie securely with heavy string. Brown meat over medium heat with oil, onion, whole garlic, and basil. Add to basic spaghetti sauce and cook until sauce and meat are done.

Savoia's Italian Beef

Tony and I spent many evening at Savoia's Restaurant in Chicago Heights when we were dating. After a show we would always drive over to the restaurant to have a beef sandwich. The Bamonti family owned the restaurant for generations. Grace, the mother, cooked and also entertained at the organ on weekends. Sylvia and Marie greeted the customers and were the "marketing specialists". Rudy handled the kitchen and Augie managed the restaurant. The cooks in the kitchen didn't have a culinary degree hanging on the wall, and some cooks hadn't gone to school beyond eighth grade, but the food that came out of that kitchen could match any of Maggiano's restaurants – maybe even Charlie Trotters. It was Italian cooking at its best. The beef sandwich was a small part of what was available at Savoia's. Veal Piccata, beef tenderloin, roast potatoes, and pasta dishes of every shape and size were served seven days a week.

Shortly after I married, I wanted to impress my husband with my culinary knowledge – even though I was incredibly inexperienced. My cousin Joanne came over one Sunday morning and helped me season the roast. To this day when I am making sirloin tip roast I follow the same procedure that Joanne showed me that Sunday in 1956.

Preparing Italian Beef With Juices

1 x 8 to 9lb. top sirloin butt or sirloin tip roast

garlic clove

4oz. oil

6oz. Rhine wine

salt and pepper

3 sprigs parsley

1 cup warm water

1 small onion

3 stalks celery

Make slits in the meat, and insert parsley, garlic, salt and pepper. Place meat in pan and rub oil over meat. Braise meat in oven at 400 degrees, turning frequently during browning process. Decrease oven to 375 degrees.

Add celery, garlic, parsley, onion, water and wine. Cook uncovered for 2½ hours, basting occasionally. This will be a medium rare roast beef. Remove from oven and let cool for about 15 to 20 minutes. Slice with a meat slicer to desired thickness.

Juice for beef:

Remove meat from pan. Keep warm. Skim off excess fat or oil from pan. Add more wine and water, if necessary. Place on top of stove and cook slowly, scraping bottom and sides of pan to collect all of the juices from the cooking process. Salt and pepper to your taste. Add beef to juice as needed for sandwiches. Serve with hard rolls.

Italian Meatball Sandwich

½ lb. ground beef

½ ground pork

1 cup seasoned breadcrumbs

½ cup grated Parmesan or Romano cheese

¼ cup minced parsley

2 eggs, well beaten

salt and pepper to taste

¼ cup olive oil

2 cloves garlic, cut in half

Mix the ingredients and shape into small balls about 1" in diameter. Heat olive oil and garlic in skillet. Add meatballs and brown on all sides, turning occasionally. Remove meatballs from skillet and drain well on paper towels. Add to sauce about 15 minutes before the sauce is done. Place the meatball with a little sauce on a hard roll.

You will need extra paper napkins for this sandwich.

Stuffed Pork Roast

1 x 5lb. Pork Loin Roast

1 box Stovetop Chicken stuffing, prepared according
   to directions on box

1 whole apple, peeled, cored and chopped

2 stalks of celery, chopped

Preheat oven to 375 degrees. With sharp knife, cut 2 thick slices through roast lengthwise, three-quarters of the way through, being careful not to cut all the way through. Prepare stuffing, adding apple and celery, then mix thoroughly. Spread dressing on opened roast, leaving ½-inch border around the sides. Fold the roast over, enclosing the filling. Tie with a string to secure roast. Place in oven in roaster with low sides or in a Pyrex baking dish, and roast for 45 minutes. Insert meat thermometer in center of meat and continue to roast until meat thermometer reads

155 degrees. Let stand for 15 minutes to set juices. Remove the string from the meat and slice meat in ½ inch slices. I prepare this dish as a large buffet entrée.

Mom's Beef Stew

3lb. sirloin steak cut in 2" cubes	6 tablespoons oil
2 medium chopped onions	1 clove chopped garlic
salt and pepper to taste	4 large carrots cut in chunks
3 stalks chopped celery	6 medium potatoes, quartered
2 bouillon cubes	4 cups hot water
1½ cups dry red wine	1 x 8oz. canned tomatoes, mashed with juice

In a large pot, brown meat, garlic, chopped onions in oil until meat is browned. Add salt, pepper, carrots, potatoes, and celery. Allow to steam for about 15 minutes. Blend the bouillon cubes with the water and pour into the pot with the wine. Bring to boil, and then reduce heat. Cover and cook slowly for about 1½ hours or until vegetables are tender. If the gravy for stew is too thin, add 1 tablespoon of cornstarch that has been diluted in 1 cup of warm water.

Serve with hot rolls.

Roast Pheasant with Dressing

1 dressed pheasant, about 2½ lbs

2 to 3 slices bacon

1 box Stovetop Stuffing for Chicken

salt and pepper to taste

1 to 2 tablespoons oil

Remove the extra pinfeathers by plucking them with tweezers or by hand. Singe the pheasant over a low flame to remove any extra feathers from the bird. Wash thoroughly and dry the pheasant thoroughly, and then salt the inside lightly. Using the prepared Stovetop Stuffing for Chicken, pack dressing loosely in bird. Wrap heavy string around the stuffed area and then place on a low-sided roasting pan with one or two tablespoons of oil on the bottom of the roasting pan. Place bacon on top of pheasant. Roast at 325 degrees. Cover the pheasant and bake for 1 hour then uncover to brown the pheasant. When the pheasant is crisp and brown, remove from oven and cool for a few minutes, then scoop out the dressing, remove the bacon and cut the pheasant in half. Place the roast pheasant on a bed of stuffing and serve with vegetables or rice.

Note: Depending on the size of the bird – adjust your roasting time. You don't want to dry out the bird.

Beef Tenderloin

When I was younger, Tony's Uncle Al Tribo, who was a butcher by trade, taught me how to trim meat. This wonderfully patient man never cracked a smile when I not only cut the meat, but my hand as well.

Depending on the number of guests, you can have the butcher prepare a smaller cut of the tenderloin, however, the tenderloin is generally packaged whole. You can cut the amount you need at home and freeze the rest. After the tenderloin is trimmed, place in the oven on a roasting pan with low sides. I have even used a large, sturdy cookie sheet to roast the tenderloin.

To roast the filet, heat the oven to 450 degrees. Season the filet well with salt and pepper and other spices of choice. In a roasting pan, place 6 tablespoons of oil and coat the filet on all sides. Roast in oven for about 20 to 25 minutes, turning halfway through to brown both sides. At the end of 20 minutes, insert a meat thermometer into the center of roast – it should read 125 degrees to be served rare. Remove from oven before it reaches 140 degrees because the roast continues to cook after removal from the oven. Allow the tenderloin to relax for about 10 minutes before you slice it. This roast can be served as a buffet entrée with small rolls or as the entrée for a dinner party with roast potatoes and mushrooms; topped with a simple wine sauce. Very Elegant!

Deep Fried Calamari

Every Christmas our daughter Laurie cleaned calamari with Grandma Rendina (my mom). I remember the two of them standing at the kitchen sink cleaning pounds and pounds of calamari. Today you can go into a store, and they are already cleaned and packaged. If you are going to prepare them make sure you check the label to make sure you get the ones that are cleaned unless you want to stand over your sink and clean them. Our family couldn't have Christmas Eve without them. Last year Anne and Joe cooked the calamari in a turkey fryer and it was wonderful. They might have the job forever.

5lbs whole calamari, cleaned   flour for coating the calamari

oil for deep fryer

After you have thawed the calamari, check to see that the tubes are clear of particles. The tentacles should be free of any hard particles too. Dry thoroughly with paper towels to prepare for the fryer. Immediately before dipping in the very hot deep fryer, coat the pieces with flour. If you coat the calamari earlier and let it set, the flour doesn't stick to the calamari the way it should. Do not fry a bunch at a time, but fry a few pieces in order for the calamari to fry completely. Drain well on paper towels and serve with a cocktail sauce and sliced lemon.

Everyone fries calamari differently, but I have found, after much trial and error, that the procedure I used above works best for the cooking process.

Special Pasta Dishes

Special Pasta Dishes

Lasagna, spaghetti, manicotti, ditalini, and ravioli are only a small part of the pasta phenomenon. Noodles, shells, long strings, puffy squares or flat, wide noodles. They are all pasta. Pasta should never be cooked too long, but cooked "al dente" so that it can be felt "under the tooth". Baked, boiled or layered in rigatoni or lasagna dishes, served with oil and garlic, various tomato sauces, or just plain butter, pasta is a large part of Italian cuisine.

In Italy, the restaurants don't drown their pasta dishes in sauce. There is usually a light covering of sauce over the pasta so that you can enjoy not only the sauce but the pasta as well. Many older Italians make a heavy sauce. I prefer a light tomato sauce with fewer spices. It is easier on the digestive system.

Manicotti

The very first time I made manicotti, I prepared it for a business party Tony was having in the back yard at our house on St. Joseph Avenue in Kankakee. During that era, he and Dick Ackman would invite all of the elected officials in the county, and I would cook for the party. Some years we entertained over a hundred people. It was always held in our back yard, and the menu pretty much remained the same.

Then one year, an Italian cookbook from Saint Rocco Church in Chicago Heights was given to me as a gift. I found the recipe for manicotti, and I decided to add it to the menu. Well, it was a big hit and we continued to prepare manicotti, rib eye steaks, tossed salad and tomato bread with plenty of liquid refreshments.

I have prepared hundreds and hundreds of these delectable crepes. As complicated as they might look to prepare, they are quite easy. Sometimes even easier than stuffing the store bought shells –mainly because the shells break apart easily.

Our daughter Beth found a recipe for spinach manicotti and that too has become part of our tradition, especially at Christmas. So the next time you want to try something special for a dinner party, try making the manicotti crepes. You and your guests won't be sorry that you did.

Preparing and Assembling the Manicotti

Filling:

3lbs. ricotta cheese

4 eggs

1 teaspoon salt

¼ teaspoon pepper

¼ cup parsley

Pancake:

6 eggs

3 cups water

3 cups flour

1 teaspoon salt

½ cup Parmesan cheese

Beat eggs and gradually add water and salt. Add the flour and beat, as you would pancake flour until light and smooth. Grease an electric frying pan with butter or you can use a pan that you can easily manipulate. Pour a little batter in the pan to cover the bottom, trying to make the pancake as thin as possible without breaking it. Flip the pancake and cook both sides. Continue to do this until all of the batter has been used, setting the pancakes aside to be filled. In a Pyrex baking dish, ladle enough sauce to cover the bottom of the dish. Meanwhile, place a small amount of filling in the center of each pancake and roll. Place the pancake seam side down on the Pyrex dish. Ladle a small amount of sauce on each pancake and place in oven. Bake at 325 degrees until heated through, approximately 20 to 30 minutes.

This takes some time to prepare, but it is an elegant dish for a buffet table or a holiday. The original recipe comes from the Saint Rocco Church Cookbook.

Beth's Spinach Manicotti

Beth introduced this recipe to our family in the early 1980's. She prepared it for a dinner party that Tony and I were having for our friend Scott Darst and his family. We served this pasta dish with beef tenderloin and a mixed salad. It was a huge success and we have been using this recipe ever since then.

> 1 box frozen Stouffer's Spinach Soufflé, defrosted
>
> or
>
> 1 x 10oz. package of frozen chopped spinach cooked and squeezed dry
>
> 1 cup ricotta cheese
>
> 1 cup mozzarella cheese
>
> 1 eggcup Parmesan cheese
>
> 1lb. manicotti shells
>
> salt and pepper to taste
>
> marinara sauce (p.69)

In a large pot bring water to a boil, then add manicotti. Cook al dente. Drain and cool. Separate the manicotti shells on wax paper to cool. In a mixing bowl, combine the spinach, ricotta, and ¾ cup of the Parmesan cheese. Mix well. Season with the salt and pepper. Dry the pasta shells carefully with a paper towel. Using a teaspoon, place the spinach mix into the manicotti shell. The shell may split, so handle carefully. Do not overload the shell as they do expand when baking.

Preheat oven to 350 degrees. Spread a thin layer of sauce on the bottom of a 9x13 baking dish and arrange the shells on the dish. Spoon more sauce over the shells. Sprinkle mozzarella cheese and ¼ Parmesan cheese over the sauce and bake in preheated oven for 25 minutes or until manicotti is heated through.

Baked Mostacciolli with Eggplant Mushroom Sauce

4 cups marinara sauce (p.69)

1lb. mostaccioli

1 medium eggplant

4 large fresh mushrooms, sliced

1x16oz. package shredded mozzarella cheese

oil for pan

Cut eggplant lengthwise and let them drain for about 1 hour. Then cut into chunks. Do not peel. Clean and cut mushrooms. In cast iron fry pan over medium heat, pour ¼ cup oil to cover bottom of pan. Add mushrooms and eggplant and sauté until light brown. Add to basic tomato sauce. The mushroom mix should be crisp not mushy. Boil the mostaccioli as directed on package and drain. In large bowl, mix the mostaccioli with 1 cup of sauce.

To assemble: In a 9x13 pan, spoon 1 cup tomato sauce (minus the mushrooms and eggplant) on bottom of pan. Add the pasta, Top with the eggplant and mushroom sauce. Sprinkle mozzarella cheese over the top. Bake in a 350-degree oven for 30 to 35 minutes. Tom and Anne love this dish.

Fusilli with Eggplant Sauce

Here is another variety of pasta that is served in our home all of the time. Anne came to dinner one evening when I served the spiral pasta with an eggplant sauce. She raved about the dish and now every time I serve pasta, Anne asks for this particular dish.

I have one problem with that. When I made the pasta dish, it was a last-minute thing so I didn't measure all of the ingredients. I followed the advice of my mom and aunts. I had some sauce left in the freezer, an eggplant in the fridge, and a box of the spiral pasta. So I mixed it together and served it. This pasta goes well with either marinara sauce or Grandma's basic sauce. I guess it just goes to show how versatile Italian cooking can be: *A little of this and a little of that.*

Potato Gnocchi

5lbs. Idaho potatoes

4 cups all-purpose flour

marinara sauce (p.69)

3 eggs

Parmesan cheese

Boil potatoes, then peel and put through a potato ricer. Spread on a large cutting board to cool. When the potatoes are cool, place in a large bowl and add the eggs. Mix well. Add flour slowly to make pliable dough. Cut or break off pieces and roll larger than the thickness of a pencil. You can make several "ropes" of the mix. Cut the gnocchi ropes into 2-inch pieces. Meanwhile, fill a large pot with water. Bring to a boil and drop the gnocchi into the boiling water. Cover and simmer until gnocchi comes to the surface. Taste test one for tenderness. When the gnocchi are tender, drain well and place them on a large platter. Add spaghetti sauce and grated Parmesan cheese. These are Tony, Tom, and Joe's favorites.

Ellie's Lasagna

Tony likes to describe his Aunt Kitty as, "*Auntie Mame*", like the movie character, and in a way she really was like that. She and Uncle Champ owned a restaurant called *The Ranch House*, and Tony and I spent many evenings there listening to Uncle Champ sing, and eating Aunt Kitty's wonderful Lasagna. Aunt Kitty was always in the kitchen because either the cook was sick, or the he drank too much and couldn't come to work. Any restaurant owner knows the story.

Shortly after Tony and I were married, he suggested that I learn how to make Aunt Kitty's Lasagna. So one morning I walked over to the restaurant, and Aunt Kitty very patiently taught me how to make Lasagna. She sent me home with the recipe and a tray of Lasagna. I have basically followed her recipe for the last forty-eight years.

When I married at nineteen, I could barely boil water. That's strange considering that my mom rarely left the kitchen because she was always cooking for our large family. But I was the youngest in the family and I did other menial chores – like feeding the chicken, gathering eggs from the chicken coop and dusting the legs of the large, round dining room table. I was determined to be a good cook when I married and after much trial and error, I learned how to cook – and cook well I did!

Preparing the Lasagna

1 full recipe of marinara sauce (p.69)

2lb. lasagna (you won't use it all)

2lb. ricotta cheese

3 eggs

1lb. lean ground beef

1 teaspoon salt

¼ teaspoon pepper

¼ cup parsley

½ cup grated cheese

1 x 16oz. package of shredded mozzarella cheese

Mix the Ricotta cheese, eggs, salt, pepper, and parsley and set aside. Meanwhile, heat 3 tablespoons of oil, add the ground beef and brown the meat. Drain extra grease and set aside. When meat is cool and well drained, add it to the ricotta mixture and set aside.

In a large pot bring approximately 6 quarts of water to a boil. Cook the lasagna noodles al dente. Don't overcook the noodles because they cook more when baking in the oven. Drain well and lay the lasagna strips flat on wax paper to cool.

To assemble:

Using a 9x13 baking dish, cover bottom with Grandma Rendina's sauce, and top with a layer of lasagna strips. Spread a layer of ricotta cheese with the ground meat over the strips, a thin layer of sauce and top with a layer of mozzarella cheese. Repeat layering, ending with meat sauce. Top with another thin layer of mozzarella cheese. Cover loosely with foil and bake at 350 degrees for 30 minutes. Remove the foil and bake 10 more minutes. Remove from oven and cool for 5 minutes before cutting.

Baked Rigatoni

1½ lbs. rigatoni	2 eggs
1½ lb fresh ricotta cheese	½ cup Romano cheese
1 x 16oz. package mozzarella cheese	½ cup parsley
salt and pepper to taste	marinara sauce (p.69)

Bring a large pot of water to a rolling boil. Add pasta and cook about 15 to 20 minutes, al dente, over medium heat. Drain well and set aside. In a large bowl, add ricotta, 2 eggs, salt and pepper, parsley and ½ cup Romano cheese.

Cover the bottom of a 9x13 pan with sauce, then cover the sauce with a layer of rigatoni and then spread the ricotta mixture over that. Spoon a little sauce over pasta and ricotta and repeat; ending with sauce on top. Sprinkle mozzarella cheese over the top and bake in a 350-degree oven for 35 minutes or until cheese is melted. Cut into squares and serve.

This is a variation of Lasagna –it's not as heavy. However, if you want to add ground round meat, you can add it to your marinara sauce. This is a good dish to serve for large groups as it can be made ahead of time and stored in your freezer.

Pasta Marinara and Mt. Langham Wine
Compliments of Joe Azzarelli

Joe and Barbara Azzarelli lived across the street from us when all of our kids were growing up. Unfortunately for us, Tony and I didn't really get to know Joe and Barbara until all of our kids grew up and we all moved from Marycrest in Kankakee. Joe was on the board of Area Jobs Development Association for many years while Tony was the director. In 2001, Joe's health was failing so when he and Barbara invited Tony and me to Florida to visit, we accepted. We had a really great time with Joe, Barbara, Sam and Jean. We laughed for four days. Joe wanted to go fishing badly, so one day Sam, Joe and Tony went fishing. Even with his health failing Joe wasn't ready to give up his hobbies and his friends. That evening, Sam and Joe made pasta with sauce, and true to Italian cooking; Sam made enough to feed twenty people instead of the six of us. One of Joe's favorite breakfast dishes was called "Dutch Babies". You could describe it as a large pancake. One morning while we were visiting with Barbara and some of their family, Barbara made it. It was very good! This is such a nice memory of Joe.

Linguine with Calamari Sauce

1lb. linguine½ cup light olive oil

1 x 16oz. can of tomato sauce

salt and pepper to taste

3 tablespoons chopped fresh basil

1 small jar of Ragu* traditional sauce

1lb. calamari, cleaned, drained and patted dry

½ cup red wine

Heat ¼ cup olive oil in large pot. Add tomato sauce, basil, salt and pepper to taste and cook over medium heat for 15 minutes. Add one small jar of Ragu and ½ glass of wine. Simmer on stove while you prepare the calamari.

Meanwhile in medium-sized pot, heat ¼ cup oil. Add drained calamari and sauté, stirring occasionally. The calamari will turn a light pinkish color. With slotted spoon remove the calamari from pot and add to the sauce. Simmer sauce with calamari for 30 minutes until flavors blend. If the sauce becomes too thick, add a ½ jar of water from the Ragu jar.

*Older Italian cooks who cooked their sauces for hours would probably cringe over the thought of Ragu, but I find that it gives more flavor and texture to the sauce.

Traditional Pasta Sauces

Marinara Sauce

6 large tomatoes, peeled and chopped

   or

1 large can plum tomatoes with juice and blended in food processor or blender

2 cloves of garlic cut in half. Remove before serving pasta.

1 tablespoon chopped fresh basil or 1 teaspoon dried basil

1 teaspoon chopped fresh flat-leaf parsley

salt and pepper to taste

3 tablespoons olive oil.

In a large saucepan, heat the oil and garlic. Lightly brown garlic and then add tomatoes with juice and the rest of the ingredients. Reduce heat down to low and simmer sauce until a light oil film surfaces on sauce, approximately 40 minutes. Serve over pasta of choice. Serves four.

Meatballs with Sauce

1½ lb. ground chuck

1 cup seasoned breadcrumbs

¼ cup minced parsley

salt and pepper to taste

¼ cup olive oil

½ lb. ground pork

¼ cup grated Parmesan cheese

2 eggs, well beaten

garlic, optional

marinara sauce (p.69)

Mix together the ingredients as listed and shape into small balls. Heat oil and garlic in frying pan. Add meatballs and brown on all sides, turning occasionally. Remove meatballs from pan as they brown and drain well on paper towels. Add to sauce about 15 minutes before sauce is done. You can also place the meatballs in your sauce without browning them in the skillet. It makes a softer meatball and isn't fried.

When using the meatballs for sandwiches, place two or three meatballs on an Italian roll and spoon a little of the sauce over the meatball. Messy, but oh so delicious!

Pasta with Arrabiatta Sauce

¼ cup olive oil

½ to ¾ teaspoons dried red-pepper flakes

1 tablespoon chopped fresh basil

1lb. ground round steak

2 cloves minced garlic

2 tablespoons parsley

1 x 28oz. can crushed tomatoes in puree

1lb. Penne Pasta

In large cast-iron frying pan, heat the oil over low heat. Add the garlic and cook for a few minutes or until garlic is golden. Add ground meat and brown. Add tomatoes, parsley, basil, salt and red pepper flakes and simmer for 30 to 35 minutes.

Meanwhile boil water for the pasta. Cook pasta al dente. Drain and place in large platter. Spoon the sauce over the pasta and mix to coat the pasta. Finish with a little more basil. Very good!

Arrabiatta in Italian means angry. In cooking it means spicy.

Pasta with Meat Sauce

2lbs. pork neck bones

4 Italian sausage cut in half

⅓ cup virgin olive oil

1 cup dry red wine

2 large cloves garlic

Meatballs (p. 60)

2 to 3 tablespoons fresh chopped basil

2 x 16oz. cans Hunts Tomato Sauce

1 medium jar Ragu traditional sauce

salt and pepper to taste

Heat the oil and garlic in large pot over medium heat. Add sausage and neck bones and sauté for about 15 minutes until brown. Remove the meat and set aside. Deglaze the pan with 1 cup red wine, stirring to deglaze. Add tomato sauce and cook over low heat for 20 minutes. Add Ragu sauce and simmer uncovered for 30 minutes. Add basil, sausage, and neck bones to sauce and simmer for 1 hour. Remove garlic before serving. Remove the meat to a serving platter. Serve with your choice of pasta.

Every region in Italy has its own recipe for making sauce and every Italian cook has their own version of their favorite sauce. The sauces that I enjoyed as a child were heavier than the sauces that I make now. I include the Ragu because it adds more richness and flavor to the tomato sauce without the sauce becoming too heavy.

Spaghetti Sauce Bolognese

1 cup white mushrooms

1lb. ground chuck

2 onions, chopped

¼lb. prosciutto, sliced very thin

2 tablespoons butter

2 tablespoons olive oil

4 cups canned Italian plum tomatoes

1 small can tomato paste

1lb. pasta of choice, preferably long pasta

Wash mushrooms well. Chop finely and add to raw meat in frying pan. Meanwhile, sauté onions and prosciutto in 2 tablespoons butter until onions are golden brown. Add the mixture to raw beef and mushrooms. Cook, stirring, until meat has browned. Add the tomatoes and tomato paste and continue cooking for 2 hours, simmering slowly, uncovered, until sauce is thickened.

This is a very rich sauce, but delicious.

Pasta with Oil, Garlic and Tomato

½ cup extra virgin olive oil, good quality

2 cloves garlic, minced

salt and pepper to taste

red pepper flakes

Parmesan cheese, good quality

1lb. Linguine or fettuccine

1 chopped tomato

Cook the pasta according to the directions. Drain well. In a large bowl, combine the pasta, oil and garlic. Add red pepper flakes, chopped tomato and salt to taste. Mix well. Sprinkle with cheese and serve immediately.

Delectable Desserts

Some Italian cooks produce some really elegant desserts. It used to be that desserts like ricotta-filled cannoli tubes were reserved for special occasions such as bridal parties, weddings and Christmas celebrations.

Today you can create the same delicious desserts with ease because some of the ingredients have been processed already for you. Any Italian specialty store can provide their customers with all of the tools necessary not only for delectable desserts, but the tools to create a masterpiece such as Zuppa Inglese or Strufoli. Cannoli is made easier because the tubes are already packaged for the consumer.

When traveling through Italy, Tony and I found that after an ordinary dinner, Italians prefer a light dessert of fresh fruit and a wedge of cheese.

Alba Spada's Banana Cake

Alba Spada is Tony's godmother. She not only makes a luscious banana cake, but she also is one of the great cooks that served seven-course wedding dinners in Chicago Heights for many years.

2 cups sifted cake flour	1¼ cup sugar
1 teaspoon baking powder	1 teaspoon baking soda
½ teaspoon salt	½ cup butter or margarine
¼ cup finely chopped pecans	2 eggs, well beaten
1 cup mashed ripe bananas	¾ cup whole milk
1 teaspoon vanilla	

Sift flour adding baking soda and powder. Cream butter. Add sugar, beaten eggs, and bananas. Add flour, milk, vanilla, and nuts. Bake in greased and floured 10-inch tube pan in 350-degree oven for 45 to 50 minutes. Cool completely and invert.

Frost with a light glaze or powdered sugar.

Alba had this cake baking for 50 to 55 minutes on her recipe, which I found made the cake too dry. My Viking oven baked it in 30 minutes. Depending on your stove, I suggest using an oven thermometer for the baking time.

Amaretti Cookies

1 x 8oz. can almond paste

1 cup sugar

2 large egg whites, room temperature

red or green candied cherries

Preheat the oven to 350 degrees. Line two large baking sheets with parchment paper. In a large bowl of an electric mixer or food processor, combine the almond paste and sugar. Process or beat until blended. Add the egg whites and process or beat until very smooth.

Scoop one scant tablespoon of the batter and lightly roll into a ball. You may have to dampen the tips of your finger to prevent sticking. Place on parchment paper 1 inch apart. Push a candied cherry firmly into the top of each cookie.

Bake for 18 to 20 minutes, until the cookies are lightly browned. Let cool briefly on the sheets. Gently transfer the cookies to rack or platter using a thin spatula. Store in an airtight container.

The other cookies in the picture are chocolate chip and oatmeal cookies.

Mrs. Senn's Apple Crisp

My first job after graduation was at First National Bank in Chicago Heights. It was a family-owned business and everyone there knew each other through family or schools they had attended together. Mrs. Senn was the cook in the small cafeteria and every day for around a dollar, we ate the most delicious lunches.

5 to 6 apples	1 tablespoon cinnamon
¼ teaspoon salt	

Spray 8x8 baking pan with Pam or other oil spray and set aside. Wash, core and peel apples. Slice the apples. Add cinnamon and salt. Heat oven to 425 degrees. Combine all the topping ingredients; mix with fork until crumbly and spoon over apples. Place in oven. Bake uncovered at 350 degrees for 35 to 40 minutes, or until top is golden brown.

Topping:

½ cup sugar	½ cup brown sugar
¾ cup all-purpose flour	½ cup margarine or butter

Serve warm with light whipped topping.

Cannoli

Filling:

3lbs. ricotta cheese

2½ cups milk

8 tablespoons cornstarch

1 tablespoon vanilla

1 cup semi-sweet chocolate, optional

red and green chopped maraschino cherries, optional

3 cups sugar

*24 cannoli shells

Bring milk to boil over low flame. Slowly mix in cornstarch and sugar. Remove from heat and allow to cool for 30 minutes. Meanwhile beat cheese until creamy. Add cornstarch mixture, vanilla, and beat until very fluffy. Add the cherries, and pieces of chocolate. Fill pastry shells from both ends. Sprinkle with powdered sugar. Cannoli shells can be stored and filled as needed.

*Shells can be purchased at any Italian specialty shop. Use fresh ricotta. Some packaged ricotta can be grainy.

Deluxe Cheesecake

Last year, Beth and I visited Tom in New York. After we had attended a concert in Brooklyn, Tom suggested that we walk to *Junior's* for, as he said, "The best cheesecake in New York." He told us that it was a short walk, so we proceeded to walk. After quite a hike, we arrived at *Junior's* to find the place packed. The waiter finally brought us to our table and when he delivered the massive pieces of cheesecake, we devoured every bite. I don't think we even spoke to each other as we ate. It was that good. It was worth the walk to find *Junior's* – however, we took a cab back to Tom's apartment! We probably should have taken a cab there and walked back to the apartment.

½ cup butter or margarine, softened	1½ cups sugar
3 large egg yolks	1¼ cups plus 3 tablespoons flour
5-8oz. packages cream cheese	5 large eggs
¼ cups whole milk	1 teaspoon grated lemon peel

Continued

Preheat oven to 400 degrees. In a small bowl, with mixer at low speed, beat butter and ¼ cup sugar until blended. Add 1 egg yolk and beat until well combined. Beat in 1¼ cups flour just until combined. Divide dough into almost equal parts, wrap slightly larger piece in plastic and refrigerate until needed. With hands, press smaller piece of dough onto bottom of 10-inch spring form pan. Bake until golden, about 8 minutes. Cool completely in pan on wire rack.

Turn oven up to 475 degrees. In large bowl, with mixer at medium speed, beat cream cheese until smooth, gradually beating in remaining 1¼ cups sugar. Reduce speed to low. Beat in 5 eggs, remaining egg yolks, milk, remaining 3 tablespoons flour, and lemon peel just until blended, occasionally scraping the sides of bowl with rubber spatula.

Press remaining dough around sides of pan 1-inch from rim. Pour cream cheese mixture into crust and bake 12 minutes. Turn oven down to 300 degrees and bake for 30 minutes longer. Edge will be set, but center will jiggle. Turn off oven. Let cheesecake remain in oven for another 30 minutes then remove from oven. Run knife along edges to prevent cracking while cooling. Cool completely on wire rack. Cover and refrigerate until well chilled. Remove sides of pan to serve.

Red Velvet Cake with Cream Cheese Frosting

1½ cups sugar

1⅓ Crisco oil

1 teaspoon white vinegar

2 eggs

1 teaspoon cocoa

1½ cups flour

1 cup buttermilk

1 teaspoon baking soda

1 teaspoon salt

2 small bottles red food coloring

Combine sugar and oil then add flour, salt and baking soda. Mix in buttermilk and eggs. In separate bowl, mix cocoa, vinegar, food coloring and vanilla. Add to buttermilk mixture and mix well. Pour into two round 9-inch cake pans, greased. Bake at 350 degrees for 25 to 30 minutes. Cool completely before frosting. You can also use a 9x13 baking dish for this cake instead of layering it.

Frosting:

1 stick butter

1 x 8oz. package cream cheese

1lb. powdered sugar

1 teaspoon vanilla

Mix butter, cream cheese, sugar and vanilla. Mix well.

This is our son-in-law Dan and Joe's favorite cake. My sister Dee made this all the time for her son Dan.

Terry B.'s Lemon Chiffon Pie

Pie Shell:

½ cup spry (shortening), less 1 tablespoon

3 tablespoons boiling water

1 teaspoon milk

1¼ cup sifted flour

½ teaspoon salt

Place spry in mixing bowl. Add boiling water and milk. Whip with fork until thick like whipped cream. Add flour and salt. Stir quickly with "round the bowl" strokes, forming a ball. Roll dough between 2 squares of waxed paper. Fit pastry into pan. Prick all over with fork. Bake in 450-degree oven 14 to15 minutes.

Filling:

½ cup cold water

1 tablespoon Knox gelatin

½ cup sugar

4 eggs, separated

dash of salt

½ cup sugar

⅓ cup lemon juice

Soften gelatin in cold water. Set aside. In double boiler, mix egg yolks, ½ cup sugar, salt and lemon juice. Cook over boiling water until thick. Remove from heat. Add gelatin. Cool. Beat egg whites stiff. Add ½ cup sugar gradually. Fold into cooled lemon mixture. Pour in pie shell. Cover loosely with saran wrap or wax paper. Chill. To serve, top with whipped cream or topping of choice.

Uncle Dutchs' Famous Pineapple Upside Down Cake

1 cup brown sugar	5 tablespoons pineapple juice (Reserve the juices)
3 eggs	⅛ teaspoon salt
1 cup sugar	1 cup cake flour, sifted
½ cup butter	1 teaspoon baking powder
1xNo. 2 can, sliced pineapple	Maraschino cherries, optional

Melt butter in large 9x13 baking dish. Spread brown sugar evenly in pan and arrange the pineapple slices on the sugar. In a separate bowl, beat eggs and gradually add sugar and butter. Add pineapple juice. Mix together sifted flour, baking powder and salt and add to butter mixture. Pour over pineapple slices. Bake at 375 degrees for 30 to 35 minutes. Turn cake upside down on large rectangular platter. Enjoy!

This is one of my son-in-law Dennis' favorite desserts.

Aunt Jennie's Apple Pie

Filling:

3lb. Jonathon apples, peeled and sliced

¼ teaspoon Salt

1¼ teaspoon cinnamon

1 cup sugar

Crust:

2 cups flour

⅔ cup lard

4 to 5 tablespoon cold water

1 teaspoon salt

2 teaspoon sugar

3 to 4 teaspoons butter, sliced

Mix together all filling ingredients, except butter, and set aside. Prepare crust by adding flour, salt and sugar together. Cut in lard. Slowly add 4 to 5 tablespoons cold water, 1 tablespoon at a time until dough is pliable. Divide dough in half. Roll out half of dough and place in pie dish. Add apple mix. Top with butter. Roll out second half of dough and place on top of apple mixture. Seal edges of crust. Brush top of piecrust with a small amount of milk and sprinkle with sugar. Slit openings on top of pie. Bake at 450 degrees for 15 minutes, then turn down to 350 degrees and bake for 45 minutes. Cool and serve.

Aunt Ang's Kolackys

Dough:

½lb. cream cheese

½lb. butter or margarine

2½ cups all-purpose flour

Filling:

½lb. ground walnuts   ¼lb. honey

1 teaspoon cinnamon   1 tablespoon butter, melted

Sift flour and salt. Cut in butter and cheese as for piecrust. Mix together lightly. Cut dough in half. Wrap in waxed paper and chill. Roll out on floured pastry cloth. Cut in 2½-inch squares. Spread filling. Roll and seal. Bake on ungreased cookie sheet in 350-degree oven for 20 to 25 minutes. Cool. Sprinkle with powdered sugar. (Apricot, raspberry or poppy seed filling can also be used.) Delicious. Aunt Ang was famous for her Kolacky.

This is a variation of her recipe.

Mechelle's Taffy Apple Salad

When our daughter-in-law Mechelle first became a part of our family, she always asked what she could bring for any function, and I would say, "Bring a dessert." Mechelle would always bring this delicious salad. Our kids (Joe and others) can be ruthless with their teasing, and they teased Mechelle so much that she stopped bringing the salad. However, they always had their spoons ready when we brought the salad to the table. This year I asked Mechelle to bring the salad again. Trust me, there won't be a spoonful left after the "critics" are through with it.

6 apples	1 tablespoon Apple Cider Vinegar
20oz. can of crushed pineapple	2 eggs
1 cup sugar	1 cup dry-roasted peanuts
2 tablespoons flour	1 x 16oz. cool whip

Slice apples – pour pineapple juice over apples and let stand. Mix flour, sugar, vinegar, and eggs together. Mix well. Drain the apples and add to flour mixture.

Add cool whip and crushed pineapple along with ⅓ cup crushed peanuts. Mix well. Garnish with peanuts. Refrigerate.

The Second Annual Rib Cookoff

The chef's arrived at ten a.m. on a beautiful, clear Saturday morning. The grills had been set up for the two chefs. Because they are masters of the grill, we didn't interfere with their charcoal grill wizardry. Thirty-five people were invited to taste the succulent ribs that the two masters would challenge each other with during the course of the process. And so we began.

Bob Arrigo at the grill

Donnie Vaughn at the grill

Our chefs each had their own recipe for the success of their ribs. They both used their own 'secret' recipe for the ribs. For this occasion, both men used a five-foot grill. With thirty-five to forty people invited, we needed the space to accommodate the ribs. Bob had stewed his ribs. He used a combination of three different types of pepper along with garlic and other seasonings. He then basted the ribs in his homemade sauce, adding the peppers and garlic.

Don on the other hand, did not stew his ribs. He dry rubbed them with a combination of spices and herbs and then laid them on the grill; basting the ribs as they grilled.

Both men started their grills at around 10:30 and then laid their ribs on the grill to cook slowly; basting often for several hours. At 2:30 they announced that the ribs were ready to eat. Each of the men had their own recipe for their ribs; and each one was delicious.

Everyone had a wonderful time. We all decided on a 3rd annual Rib Cookoff at a later date; but not too far in the future.

Everyone has their own recipe for grilling. Some people use a charcoal grill while others use a gas grill. Some people parboil their ribs, and some people choose to place the raw meat on the grill.

The following is the recipe for ribs that Tony and I have been using for years, which we 'borrowed' from the San Rocco Parish Cookbook in Chicago Heights, Illinois.

8 to 10lb back ribs
salt and pepper to taste
3 cups of water
1 cup wine vinegar

After coals have turned white, place ribs about 10 to 12 inches from coals on the grill.
Meanwhile, combine the following ingredients in a saucepan.

2 bottles catsup (I use Heinz)
4oz. tarragon vinegar
1 bottle Chilli Sauce
1 lemon cut in quarters
½ bottle Worcestershire sauce
½ cup brown sugar
4oz. water
1 teaspoon dry mustard
Tabasco sauce

Holiday Traditions

When Mom told us to go into the attic and bring down the old black trunk with all the Christmas ornaments, my siblings and I knew that it was time to start decorating for Christmas. For our family Christmas preparations didn't begin the day after Thanksgiving; they began when Mom and Dad had enough money to purchase a tree, some presents, and food for the holiday. It certainly didn't start after Halloween, as it does in many department stores. There was a time and place for everything when I was a youngster and the time for celebrating Christmas was December.

The first thing our family did was to get the house ready for Christmas. This meant washing windows, cleaning carpets, washing walls and cleaning "everything" because in my mom's mind, we were preparing as though company was coming to stay for a week. After the house was shining clean, we put up the tree. The ornaments had been saved from year to year and they were hung with great care. I always had the job of hanging the tinsel, a tedious job, and one I noticed that the older kids in my family always relegated to the youngest sibling.

The holiday season reached a crescendo at either Christmas Midnight Mass or Christmas Morning Mass. As a child, we went to church Christmas morning, either taking a bus, or one year, walking to St. Agnes Church. When I reached my teens, I was able to go to Midnight Mass. I can remember being so tired from our Christmas Eve feast I could barely keep my eyes open. However, when the organ struck the first chord of Silent Night, the dimmed church became aglow with candles, and the priest began his descent down the aisle, I woke up. The smell of incense, mixed with the floral scents filled the air. The altar was ablaze with dozens of rich, red poinsettia plants and the voices from the choir loft filled the room. Invariably, a light snow would be falling as we left church at one a.m. After greeting friends and relatives, we all went back to the house for coffee and Christmas cookies before we went to bed.

At that time, Christmas morning was very different than the Christmas mornings that I share with my family now. While we have maintained the tradition, the quantity of gifts is very different. Christmas shopping wasn't a priority while I was growing up, probably because there were many money issues in those days, for many families.

How Mom and Dad pulled it off is still a mystery to me, but somehow my parents always made sure there was something under the tree for everyone. Today we go into overkill when it comes to buying gifts. At least I do.

Several weeks before Christmas, I pull down the round tin containers that have been stored from prior years. My recipes never change – almond crescents, thumbprint cookies, lemon bars, and cream cheese brownies are staples. Like Mom, I store the cookies in containers to be shared with friends and family during the holidays. The wonderful scents of cinnamon, nutmeg, and chocolate float from the kitchen, as I get ready for the holidays. The large pot of marinara sauce bubbles on the stove, and the mixture of scents fill the air.

Every year our family gathers at our home for Christmas Eve and through Christmas dinner the next day. We eat the same traditional meals that my parents and relatives served for over fifty years. While I don't have the same black trunk that mom used for the ornaments, I do have ornaments that I have saved from my children and even a few from my grandkids. Some still bear the glue from small, loving hands.

This year, our granddaughter Hannah helped to bake batches of cookies. We filled the tins with chocolate chip cookies and other traditional treats. The fish was ordered from the market, the silver was polished, and the beautiful glass Christmas dishes began to surface in anticipation of the luscious traditional food that would fill them. The tree was placed near a window, its lights twinkling between the fragrant green branches.

Several years ago, we began a ritual in our family that originated in England. "Crackers" are the brightly wrapped tubes that are filled with plastic toys and silly paper hats. Each person holds a cracker with the person sitting next to them, so everyone is connected. At once everyone pulls on the cracker and they make the sound by which they were named. The paper hats found inside have become a huge part of our Christmas Eve celebration. My kids tease me about this practice, especially because I insist that they wear the hats for a picture, but if I decided not to place the "crackers" at each place setting, they would be upset. Traditions are essential in our growing Italian family. Somehow I know that the time-honored Calamari will be at each Christmas celebration in future years.

Each year we open our door to our kids' friends and sometimes a member of our extended family that doesn't have the wonderful luxury of having a large family as Tony and I do. We try to leave our differences at the back door in order to spend a few days together sharing and caring about each other.

Last year we had a new face at our table with Ricardo; Tom's partner. This year we will have another new face at our table with the newest member of the family, Giovanna Mechelle, courtesy of Joe and Mechelle. God willing, we can continue the tradition.

Hopefully you will enjoy this cookbook as much as I have enjoyed writing it. While we all have our own history and traditions, I thank you for allowing me to share mine with you.

Buona Fortuna!

Quote

Family is at the center of life's meaning.

Individuals linked together by a golden chain of love,

Family celebrates triumphs and shares adversities across

generations and across miles.

Like a never-ending hug,

Family encircles each member with steadfast devotion

and enduring love.

Family is belonging to and believing in each other.

End Quote